DK READERS is a compelling reading _____ ne for children. The programme is designed in con, ction with leading literacy experts, including Cliff Moon M.Ed., who has spent many years as a teacher and teacher educator specializing in reading. Cliff Moon has written more than 160 books for children and teachers. He is series editor to Collins Big Cat.

Beautiful illustrations and superb full-colour photographs combine with engaging, easy-to-read stories to offer a fresh approach to each subject in the series. Each DK READER is guaranteed to capture a child's interest while developing his or her reading skills, general knowledge, and love of reading.

The five levels of DK READERS are aimed at different reading abilities, enabling you to choose the books that are exactly right for your child:

**Pre-level 1:** Learning to read
**Level 1:** Beginning to read
**Level 2:** Beginning to read alone
**Level 3:** Reading alone
**Level 4:** Proficient readers

The "normal" age at which a child begins to read can be anywhere from three to eight years old. Adult participation through the lower levels is very helpful for providing encouragement, discussing storylines and sounding out unfamiliar words.

No matter which level you select, you can be sure that you are helping your child learn to read, then read to learn!

## DK

LONDON, NEW YORK, MUNICH,
MELBOURNE, and DELHI

**Series Editor** Deborah Lock
**Designer** Jemma Westing
**Production Editor** Sean Daly
**Picture Researcher** Rob Nunn
**Jacket Designer** Natalie Godwin

**Reading Consultant**
Cliff Moon, M.Ed.

First published in Great Britain by
Dorling Kindersley Limited
80 Strand, London WC2R 0RL

10 9 8 7 6 5 4 3 2 1
001-182474-August 2011

A CIP catalogue record for this book
is available from the British Library

ISBN: 978-1-40537-639-6

Printed and bound in China by L Rex Printing Co., Ltd.

The publisher would like to thank the following for their kind
permission to reproduce their photographs:
a=above, b=below/bottom, c=centre, l=left, r=right, t=top

**Alamy Images:** Arcticphoto 21br; blickwinkel / Linke 25br;
Rosemary Calvert 24bl; Frans Lanting Studio 22; Wayne Lynch / All
Canada Photos 30-31; William Sutton / Danita Delimont 1. **Corbis:**
Daisy Gilardini / Science Faction 2br, 20; Frans Lanting 27; Norbert
Wu / Science Faction 4. **FLPA:** Tui De Roy / Minden Pictures 5;
Norbert Wu / Minden Pictures 6. **Getty Images:** Digital Vision /
David Tipling 8-9; The Image Bank / Doug Allan 18; Photographer's
Choice / Sue Flood 3; Photographer's Choice RF / Martin Ruegner
11tl; Stone / Johnny Johnson 7br. **National Science Foundation,
USA:** 29tr. **naturepl.com:** 23br; Bryan and Cherry Alexander 29bl;
Suzi Eszterhas 32crb; Fred Olivier 2cr, 10, 12, 14-15, 16, 17br, 19;
Reinhard / ARCO 24-25. **NHPA / Photoshot:** A.N.T. Photo Library
13, 17tr, 32cla; Franco Banfi 7t; Rod Planck 32bl; John Shaw 23tr;
David Tipling 2tr, 9tr, 26; Woodfall / Steve Austin 21tr. **Science
Photo Library:** British Antarctic Survey 28; Art Wolfe 11b.
**Jacket images:** Front: Getty Images: Stone / Art Wolfe.

All other images © Dorling Kindersley
For further information see: www.dkimages.com

Discover more at
# www.dk.com

# DK READERS

BEGINNING TO READ ALONE
2

# Emperor Penguins

Written by Deborah Lock

DK

A Dorling Kindersley Book

Brrr!
It is January, and the sun shines on
the icy landscape of Antarctica.
On the edges of the ice,
Emperor penguins look out to sea.

## Antarctica

Antarctica is the most southerly continent. It's a huge area of land covered in ice and snow. It is so cold that the ocean around it freezes for some of the year, making it even bigger.

Summer          Winter

They are the tallest and heaviest of all penguins.

Their thick layers of shiny, waterproof feathers keep them warm and dry.

Slide! Splash!
Penguins are birds but
they cannot fly.
Instead, they are great swimmers.
Their wings are flat and stiff
like flippers.
They dive in search of fish,
squid and krill to eat.

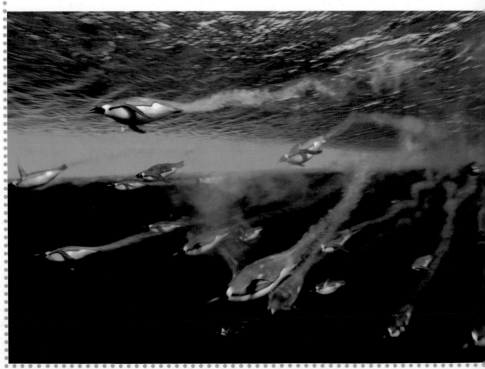

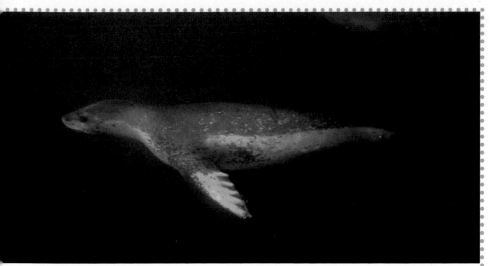

Watch out!
Leopard scals lurk under
the edges of the ice
ready to ambush them.
With a speedy leap on to
the ice, the penguins
are safe again.

At the end of March, the penguins
begin their long trek inland.
They are well fed as they will not
return to the ocean to eat
for a long time.
They waddle across the ice,
one after the other in a line.

### Tobogganing

Penguins not only waddle, but they also slide across the ice, using their flippers and feet to push their bodies along.

They have a long way to go to get to their nesting area on the firm, thick ice.

Emperor penguins gather together in colonies and there could be more than 500,000 penguins in each colony.

It is a noisy place to be because they all sing to each other.

A male penguin tries to attract a female with his voice.

If she is attracted, she will follow the male around and mate with him.

In the middle of May, the mum
lays one large pear-shaped egg.
She is tired and hungry.
She shuffles close to the dad and
very carefully passes the egg
on to his feet.
The egg must not touch
the freezing ice.

He covers the egg with
his thick, warm layers
of feathers.
The mum starts
out again on
the long journey
back to the icy
ocean.

All is quiet at the colony.
It is June, which is wintertime
in Antarctica.
The temperature drops to below
-60°C (-76°F) and the icy winds
whip around the penguins.

The dads huddle together in
a large group to keep warm.
The ones on the outside shuffle
slowly around the edge.
They take turns to be in
the middle and on the outside.

For one month, there is
total darkness.
The sky is lit up with the colourful
streaks of the Southern Lights.

## Southern Lights

The Aurora Australis, or Southern Lights, is an amazing light show in the sky. The light is made by electrical particles from the Sun entering the Earth's atmosphere and colliding with the air.

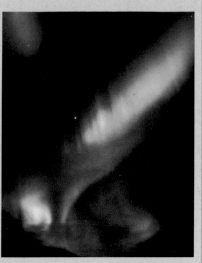

Each dad balances his egg on top of his feet to keep it warm. From time to time, the dad turns the egg very carefully, so that each part gets a chance to be the farthest away from the ice.

It is August, and the sun begins
to shine for a few hours each day.
The young chicks start to hatch
out of their eggs.

They are hungry and call for food.
The dads have not eaten
for more than 100 days and
they are hungry, too.
When will the mums return?

After nine weeks away, the mums
appear at last.
During the winter, they have
eaten well and then travelled all
the way back to the colony.

## Caring parents

Adult penguins feed their chicks by bringing back up the food they swallow. Fish can be kept fresh in their stomachs for several days. Some parts of the food become a paste or rich oil after a while.

Each dad passes his baby chick over to its mum.
He needs to be quick since the freezing ice will kill the chick within two minutes.
The chick can have a good meal at last from its mum.

The colony is a noisy place once again.
The dads leave and it's now the mums' turn to care for their fluffy young chicks.

## Dangers

The young chicks face many dangers. They could die from cold or from hunger. They could also be attacked by Southern Giant Petrels.

As they get bigger, the chicks start to waddle around and huddle together for warmth. Then it's time for their mums to leave again to get more food. The chicks are left alone for the first time.

The dads return from
their trek to the ocean
and back.
But how will they each find
their own chick?

The colony is very noisy as
the hungry chicks call out
for their dads.
Each dad calls too and then
listens out for his own chick's call.
It may take hours wandering
among the thousands of chicks
for a dad to find his baby chick.

Piu! Piu!

The mums and dads shuttle to and fro to the ocean for food for themselves and their chicks. As the sun shines longer each day, the thin ice melts and the trek to the ocean gets shorter and shorter. By November, the ocean is only a short distance away from the penguin colony.

Each new family can spend more time together.

The chicks are almost as big as their
parents now.
Their grey, downy feathers
begin to fall out and new shiny
waterproof feathers take their place.
This is called moulting.

## Moulting

During December, adult penguins also moult. They cannot swim until their new shiny waterproof feathers have grown.

Their mums and dads leave them for the last time to go and feed. The chicks will soon be ready to leave the colony, too.

*An adult's waterproof feathers*

It is January, and the sun shines
all day, every day.
There is no darkness.
For the first time, the young
penguins shuffle across
the shiny ice sheets.

They head for the shimmering
blue ocean.
They are hungry and eager for
their first dip into the icy ocean
to catch food for themselves.
Slide!

Splash!

Dive!

# Penguin facts

There are 17 different types of penguin. They all live in the southern half of the world, but some prefer warmer climates than others. The most common types are African penguins that live on the southern coast of Africa and Humboldt penguins that live on the western coast of South America.

Adelie penguins are the smallest penguins that live in Antarctica. Their black and white coloured markings make them look as if they are wearing dinner jackets.

Chinstrap penguins live in Antarctica and on the Southern Islands nearby. They have a black band of feathers under their chin that looks like a strap.

Macaroni penguins live on the islands around Antarctica. They have colourful yellow feathers on top of their heads.